CAREER 3.0:

CAREER PLANNING ADVICE TO FIND YOUR DREAM JOB IN TODAY'S DIGITAL WORLD

Contents

Disclaimer 3

Introduction 4

Your Dream Job Road Map 7

Define Yourself and Choose Your Path 15

Effective Job Search Weapons 29

Access the Invisible Job Market 42

Effective Networking 65

Resume, Cover Letters and Job Applications 86

Ace the Interview 110

Choosing Between Jobs 124

Negotiate the Final Deal 137

Mastering Your Job 149

Conclusion 165

Appendix 1(Interview Template) 166

Appendix 2(Sample Interview Template-Filled) 170

Disclaimer

Copyright © 2016

All Rights Reserved

All rights reserved. This book or any portion thereof may not be reproduced or used in any manner whatsoever without the express written permission of the publisher except for the use of brief quotations in a book review.

The information in this book is intended to provide useful information on the topics mentioned. Great care has been taken to ensure that the details in this book are accurate and up-to-date. However, the authors do not assume responsibility for any incorrect information that may be in this book. This includes information that is out of date.

Introduction

The famous comedian Drew Carey once said, "Oh, you hate your job? Why didn't you say so? There's a support group for that. It's called *everybody* and they meet at the bar." There's a great deal of truth to this.

According to a poll by the Society of Human Resource Management in 2015, around one in three Americans said they wanted to leave their job within the next six months. Forty-three percent said they would quit their job if a better opportunity arose and 28 percent said they had already quit their job. (Ref Article" "1 in 3 workers Want to Quit, HR Better Figure Out Why"

There are several reasons a person might hate their career. Most of these are factors outside the control of the employee, such as poor company management, lack of career advancement, boring work, or too much work. Many of these factors can be dealt with by changing jobs or complaining to human resources; however, a lot of them are career or industry related and you might end up facing the same problems in a different job under different management.

What if you could prevent this from happening by choosing a field that you are compatible with and one that is compatible with you? Research the jobs you want by getting all the job details beforehand, understanding your strengths and interests, and learning from the experiences of others.

With a combined 30 years of industry and job search experience, the authors of this book have composed a road map to get you to your dream job or career. Having been through this ourselves, we understand the need for a book like this. If you have any questions, please do not hesitate to contact us at modernjobsgalore@gmail.com.

Congratulations on obtaining this book. It's the first step to getting the job of your dreams. Every great achievement starts off with a well-articulated plan. And because the job hunt can be a chaotic mess, it takes a lot of planning to map out your interests and skills with the job market.

Your Dream Job Road Map

Organizing information in a systematic way is generally seen to be an incredibly boring aspect of our daily lives. Whether it's organizing a grocery list, making a list of projects at work, or even a simple list of things to do over the weekend, it's not a part of the day we look forward to. However, organization is a key to success in both our business and personal lives. Making sense of the chaos in our personal and professional lives and simplifying everything down to a list of items is the first step in taking control of your life.

In the same way, the modern job search is a chaotic mess. With millions of job listings and job seekers exhausting multiple online and offline sources, it can be an intimidating proposition for many people. Most rely on popular job forums such as CareerBuilder.com and Monster.com to avoid the greater mess around. They often apply to every single job they find online and clutch at straws. Few rely entirely on their network or newspapers.

Through 30 years of combined job search experience, the authors of this book have come up with a road map to help organize your personal job search. We will take into account your current dreams, skills, needs, and network as well as the current job market and combine these to greatly improve your job prospects.

Each aspect of this road map will be explained in detail throughout the book, we'll also include insider secrets on how to prepare for interviews, how to access the invisible job network and how to negotiate your job – all of which will be of incredible value to your job hunt.

There are nine steps in this job road map:

1. **Determine what type of job you are interested in**

    You will need to look at all the previous jobs you've held. If you're looking to land your first job, review class projects. Determine what you've enjoyed the most about each project. For example, if you loved your accounting class, you might be interested in positions where problem solving, working with numbers or working with money are major parts of your duties. List everything that you've enjoyed about each job or project. You might find that there are common elements in your previous experiences. Keep it simple and make a list of the top five items you're most interested in.

2. **Research relevant industries**

   Determine which industries match your interests. For example, working with money would indicate a career in business or finance, while working with numbers can be used in a broad array of engineering fields.

3. **Complete a skills matrix**

   Investigate a few jobs in your industries of choice that match your interests and passions. Using a skills matrix, determine what skills you possess and what skills you need to learn. Set up a training plan for the skills you must master. Examples of these are seen in later chapters.

4. **Update your resume and portfolio**

   Update your resume so that the skills you value also match with your dream job and are clearly highlighted. For example, if you love accounting because you currently work with money and you have previous experience working with money, expand on the project or position in your resume. We would also recommend a one-page description of the project or projects in your portfolio. Your portfolio should reflect all the experiences that the job requires.

5. **Reach out to your current network**

   Talk to your friends, family and acquaintances to see if they know people in your industries of interest. Complete an informational interview with these contacts to learn more about the position. Ask them for jobs that might be available.

6. **Access the invisible job market**

   Eighty percent of the job market is hidden and jobs are not always posted on public job boards. Through your network and the tips provided in this book, you will learn how to access the jobs that will give you an edge.

7. **Apply for jobs**

   Apply for jobs that are a good fit for your future goals and skills using your updated resume and portfolio.

8. **Interview**

   Be prepared for the job interview with groundbreaking tips provided in this book that will help you land the job you deserve.

9. **Negotiate and accept the job**

Use the key negotiation tools in this books to get the best possible salary for your skill set.

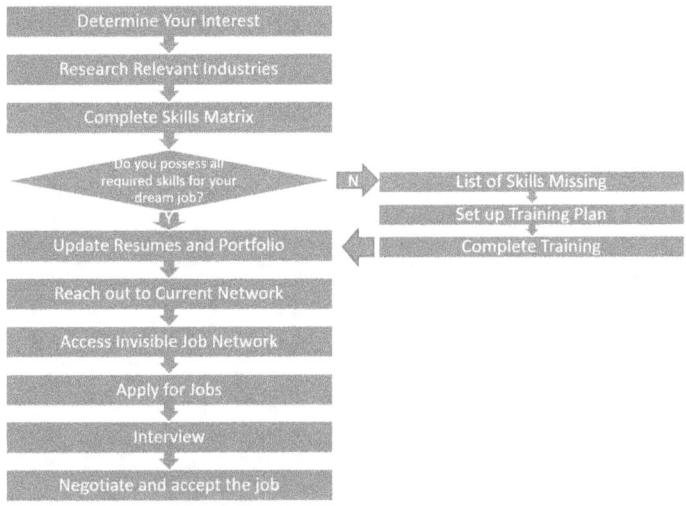

The hardest step to implement any plan is the first step. You have to take it. Once you do that, you are well on your way to achieving your goals. In the job search roadmap, the first step in this plan is the fun part. You get to determine what you want to do, figure out your interests and then you match it up with industry trends.

Define Yourself and Choose Your Path

Choosing your industry

Which industry should you choose? This is the million-dollar question. Many highly successful people seem to have fallen into a field by chance, but given the technology available today, it's much easier to analyze the different available fields and find your dream career. Ask the following questions in your decision-making process, then come up with a list of careers and sort them out by your level of interest.

- Which careers are growing?
    - Career databases, such as Onet (www.onetonline.org), have a list of all

the industries along with growth rates and average salaries

- o Google search "fastest growing careers"
- Which careers are you passionate about?
  - o Which courses did you enjoy most at school?
  - o What did you enjoy doing the most at your last job?
- Which careers closely relate to your previous experiences?
  - o What skills do job positions in different careers require?
  - o What transferable skills do you have that can be used in those jobs?
- Which careers do your family and friends work in?

- These are the industries in which you already have a foot in the door

What are the essential skills for the career?

Search for 10 jobs that you're most interested in using sources like Monster.com, LinkedIn and CareerBuilder.com. It's important that these jobs interest you. Then make a list of the skills you need for each of these jobs. Be sure to include the number of years of experience required per position. From this list, determine which are the skills you actually possess, then fill in the skills matrix included below.

	Job 1	Job 2	Job 3	Job 4	Job 5
Skill 1					
Skill 2					
Skill 3					
Skill 4					
Skill 5					
Skill 6					
Skill 7					
Skill 8					
Skill 9					
Skill 10					

Skills Matrix (unfilled)

What skills do you have?

Create a list titled "Skills I Have," these are skills you should emphasize in your resume and portfolio. Then make a list of interview stories for these experiences using the "STAR" format. These stories are experiences you have had that clearly demonstrate utilization of these skills.

What skills do you need to train for?

You will also need to create a list titled "Skills I Need," this will form the basis of your training plan. If a required skill in the job posting requests a degree, such as a Bachelors' of Science in Engineering, then you will need to look at getting a degree. If a required skill in the job posting asks for a certain number of years of experience, there are several ways to catch up and gain experience to impress the employers. Here are a few ideas to get your started:

- Do a few pet projects that demonstrate your expertise and document them clearly. You'll have to be able to explain them in the "STAR" interview format.
- Apply to internships in your area of expertise.
- Volunteer your skills to employers in the industry that interests you.

Let's look at an example: Bob has been a mechanical engineer for five years and is looking to make a career shift into a new field. Let's join Bob through the steps we just discussed that will give him direction in his selection.

Step 1: Choose your industry

- *Which fields are growing?*

    Bob visits www.onetonline.org and spends a few days researching which fields are growing. He discovers that computer analysts, wind engineers and programmers are some of the fastest growing careers with 10 to 15 percent growth per year and have a healthy median salary.

- *Which careers are you passionate about?*

  Bob has been interested in computers and programming since high school, but he instead chose a career in mechanical engineering.

- *Which careers closely relate to your previous experience?*

  Bob can use some of his mechanical engineering skills as a wind engineer, especially in building infrastructure around windmills. He has also done several projects programming machines for his previous company.

- *Which careers do your friends and family work in?*

  Bob's close friends work as programmers in different industries, so he calls them and asks them about the pros and cons of their jobs. He also hosts an informational interview with a solar engineer and a computer analyst and asks them a variety of questions about the job and the industry.

As you can see, Bob has completed extensive research into what his preferred career should be. Based on his research, he is confident that he should become either a wind engineer or a programmer. Ultimately, he decided against pursuing a career as a computer analyst because he has little experience from his current field and he is more passionate about the other two fields.

While conducting informational interviews, Bob realizes that as a computer programmer he can move between multiple industries based on his interests. He could program wind mills later on, if needed. For now, he moves on to step two.

Step 2: What are the essential skills?

The next step for Bob is to complete a skills matrix. He looks up five different job postings on CareerBuilder.com and creates a list of requirements. He enters each requirement into the skills matrix, as shown below.

	Software Net Programmer	Programmer Analyst/Entry Level	Tool Maker / CNC Programmer	Senior Programming Analyst	Programmer Analyst
Skill 1	VB. Net (2 years)	C# .Net		SSIS	.Net
Skill 2	ASP.Net	Asp. Net		Pearl	SQL
Skill 3	MVC	MVC		Python	SharePoint
Skill 4	JavaScript	JavaScript		JavaScript	
Skill 5	JQuery	JQuery		JBoss	
Skill 6	WCF			Tomcat	
Skill 7	Entity Framework	Entity Framework		iOS Apps	
Skill 8	CSS	HTML/CSS			
Skill 9			CNC Programming (3 years)		
Skill 10					

I Have Skill

I Need Skill

I have used skill before but am not proficient

Skills Matrix (Filled)
Bob lists all the skills he needs in red and lists the skills he currently has in green. Skills listed in brown are

the ones he has been trained in, but will need further practice or experience.

Step 3: What skills do you have?

In this step, Bob documents how his previous skills and experiences can be used for his dream job as a programmer. This is an important step for Bob as he realizes he is much closer to his goal than he initially thought. He browses through all his old projects and documents to check for work examples. He spends nearly a week completing this process.

He begins by creating a list of all the green/orange skills he possesses:

- JavaScript
- JQuery

- HTML/CSS

Then he creates a portfolio of work examples for each of the above skills. All of his skills are documented in the STAR interview format as well as in his resume (to make sure he does this right he reads Chapter 6 of this book).

Step 4: What skills do you need to train for?

This is the most difficult step for Bob. He realizes there is an incredible amount of time and effort needed to switch careers. He begins by making a list of skills he lacks and calls his friends in the field to ask them what it takes to learn them. Then he prioritizes each skill using the Skills Prioritization Matrix and comes up with a training plan.

The Skills Prioritization Matrix takes into account the number of times each required skill shows up on the skills matrix and the value (1 to 5) a seasoned professional would assign to the skill.

The skills that he requires are:

- VB .Net / C# .Net
- MVC
- Pearl
- Python
- Entity Framework
- iOS Apps SQL
- SharePoint

For the Skills Prioritization Matrix, Bob counts the number of times each skill appears on the skills matrix to find the "Skills Prioritization Matrix" for each job. He then asks his programmer friends to rank each skill in order of importance from 1 to 5. The total of both values marks the relative importance of each skill. Below is what he found.

Skill	Skills Matrix Value	Industry Value	Total Value
VB. Net	4	4	8
Python	1	4	5
Pearl	1	3	4
Entity Framework	2	2	4
iOS App	1	3	4
MVC	2	1	3
SharePoint	1	1	2

Skills Prioritization Matrix

Bob decides that he wants to start training for the first three skills before moving on to the others. He sets up a training plan, which involves attending a programming boot camp as well as completing pet projects. He is willing to pay $16,000 for the boot camp for three months; however, other alternatives he considered included learning it online for free or enrolling in a four-year college course for $80,000. Training plans will differ for different people based on their needs, their funds and their fields of interest. Make sure you take into account any costs and time associated with each option.

At this point, you (like Bob) have a good idea of what you need to train for and what skills you already have. Before you embark on the painstaking job search, have a look at what other job seekers have gone through so you are not surprised when you encounter the same. In fact, you might have already been through some of these issues. This is described in detail in Chapter 3.

Effective Job Search Weapons

In this chapter, we have chronicled some of the most common complaints from job seekers and explored several proven methods to overcome them.

Problem #1: I have applied for many jobs, but I'm not getting any interviews

There is no need to worry if you find yourself in this situation. Here are five ways you can overcome this frustration:

- **Positive linking**

    You will need to do targeted networking to become positively linked with your industry of interest. The number of your friends on Facebook or contacts on LinkedIn are not a guarantee that you will be able to network your way into the job of your dreams. Start by attending talks hosted by renowned experts, industry events and even happy hours – and don't forget to bring business cards! Usually, these people are very connected to others who might be able to help you get a job, but remember it's more important to connect with a few people with large networks. These people are typically harder to reach, but it is worth the effort. Another quick way to do this is to reach out to recruiters through LinkedIn or a recruitment agency.

- **Set up informational interviews**

    Once you've beefed up your network and connected with people of interest, arrange informational meetings (or "informational interviews" as they're typically called). This is a quick way to get into a real interview. There is a common saying that goes, "If you want an interview for a job, ask for job advice from people in that area."

- **Revamp your LinkedIn and Facebook profiles**

    Is your LinkedIn profile up-to-date? Does it highlight your accomplishments? It's critical that you put some thought into your summary statement and highlight your experiences and strengths. Likewise, if you're not proud of some photos on Facebook, now is the time to take them down and remove any tags you might not want your future employer to see.

- **Create an Applicant Tracking System (ATS)-friendly resume**

Most resumes are first read by a computer which matches keywords for the position with the applicant's resume. Therefore, it's surprising to see such a large number of resumes that are still not ATS-friendly. We suggest customizing your resume for every single job application to ensure that you can add as many keywords to it as possible. We also recommend using an online resume software to do this, which will ensure that your resume can be read by an ATS machine. As a general rule, remember that most of the formatting that makes a resume visually appealing cannot always be read by an ATS machine. This is explained in detail in Chapter 6.

- **Remodel cover letters**

   For most of us, a cover letter is an inconvenience

that we just want to get out of the way so we can complete the next application. This is a major mistake. Let's face it, most people don't meet all the requirements for every job, but the cover letter is a chance for you to shine. Remember to use as many keywords in the job description as possible. We suggest using a cover letter tool to help with this. Live Career has one such tool that can be useful.

Problem #2: I'm getting many interviews, but no job offers

In many ways, a job interview is a lot like a first date. Maybe the interviewer didn't like your perfume or cologne (by the way, don't wear perfume/cologne to an interview) or maybe you just weren't the right fit. But assuming you are the right fit for the job, here are some ways you can maximize your chances of getting an offer:

- **Bring Your Own Self (BYOS)**

    You're probably desperate to get the job – or any job – but it's important to play it cool. Have you ever noticed that the guys with all the girls are also the ones who attract even more girls? The same is true about the job hunt: if you want something too badly, you're not likely to get it. You can't come off as too desperate. Psych yourself up the right way before any interview. Tell yourself that it's not the end of the world if you don't land this job. Be confident in your own ability and remember that nobody can know it all. Prepare hard, visualize your future success and have the attitude that if you don't get the job, it simply wasn't meant to be.

- **Positive linking**

    The more people who can recommend you for a job before and after the interview, the better. Get connected with as many influential people within the company as possible. Learn about hiring managers and reach out to as many people as you can who will put in a good word for you. A lot of advertised jobs already have internal candidates shortlisted. Perhaps you landed an interview because an insider recommended you, but remember that other people can be recommended for jobs by even more powerful and influential insiders. We all like to believe that merit and qualifications always triumph, but strong human relationships are the most fundamental merit of all.

- **Active storytelling**

    Admittedly, storytelling is a hard thing to master; however, you don't have to be Steven Spielberg to do it right. If you have to think hard about stories you want to tell during the interview, it's probably too late to make a positive impression. Begin by thinking about your qualifications and accomplishments (spare some thought for your failures as well) about a week before the interview. Develop a list of likely interview questions and write out your answers to them. Frame your answers in the Problem, Solution, Result (PSR) format. Revise and revisit them often, especially before any interview.

- **Seek feedback**

    The very definition of "insanity" is "Doing the same thing over and over again and expecting different results." Always seek feedback. We've heard people say that not all interviewers are willing to provide feedback. Try to get what you can and adjust for subsequent interviews.

Problem #3: After so many rejections, I'm desperate, frustrated and unsure of myself

This is a common and natural response to Problems #1 and #2 above. The job search experience can be very challenging and, in some cases, downright frustrating. After all, bills have to be paid and won't wait for someone who will finally take a chance on you. We can relate to spending many months banging our heads against the wall in our own job search. If you find yourself in this situation, don't fret. Here are some effective weapons to maintain your sanity:

- **Growth mindset**

    The biggest asset you have during the job search is your confidence. This will be challenged several times, but you can't let it get you down. Remember that rejection is not about your ability, nor does it say anything about your future. Read biographies of the most successful people in history and you'll find they are full of rejections and failures. Beethoven, Benjamin Franklin and Thomas Edison are all examples of individuals who experienced rejection and failure. Instead of doubting yourself, try embracing rejection and look at it as an opportunity to grow stronger. Remember, success is 90% hard work and 10%

inspiration. Believe in yourself to succeed each time and don't let other people's actions determine the course of your destiny.

- **Positive linking and meetups**

    Extend yourself. Go out of your way to make new friends and reach out to people you haven't talked to in a long time. Use any downtime you have to join Toastmasters or a sports club, or get engaged in local politics if that's your thing. Join other groups with similar interests and consider visiting a career advisement center, most of these are free.

- **Volunteer**

    There's no better opportunity in life to use your time for good than when you don't have a job. Volunteer at a church or homeless shelter, or build homes with Habitat for Humanity. Not only will this increase your sense of self-worth, it might also be a stepping stone toward a new career.

- **Join a job center**

    The number of job resources available across the globe are staggering. Among them are job centers, which are available in many states. In northern California alone, there are at least four job centers located within a 20-mile radius. These centers are staffed by highly experienced professionals and most of their services are free. They provide workshops on resume writing, LinkedIn, behavioral interviewing, communication skills and other valuable information to help job seekers like yourself.

At this point, you are mentally prepared to start the job search. In the next chapter, you will learn to do what many job seekers fail at. The art of networking has always been the most important factor in getting you the right job. And gaining access to the hidden network will give you an even bigger advantage.

Access the Invisible Job Market

Are you stuck trying to find success in your job hunt? In this chapter, we'll discuss how you can quadruple your job success rate by unlocking the invisible (or hidden) job market.

What is the invisible job market?

In summer 2011, I attended an internship in Chicago. The "big boss" visited that year's cohort of interns, about 15 of us in total. He asked each of us how we found out about the internship opportunity, to which 13 said that they knew someone working at the company. He wondered aloud why almost nobody came in through the company's online application process or the many career fairs the company organized.

I was shocked by this apparent nepotism and my first response was, "I thought this only happened in poor countries like mine with high levels of corruption." However, I caught myself and my outrage quickly disappeared when I remembered that I got in because the CEO of the company gave me a personal referral.

The jobs open to most job seekers can be found by anyone on job boards like Indeed.com or Monster.com. This is the "visible job market." However, as we'll later see, these jobs account for less than 20 percent of all available jobs. The remaining jobs can be found on the "invisible job market" or the "hidden job market."

Carrie Kreuger of the Jobfully blog defines the hidden job market as "jobs that are revealed through channels other than advertisements or job board postings." Another good definition of the term from the

Simply Hired blog is "the invisible job market refers to the untold number of job openings that never appear online or on any public website."

Why you need to focus on the hidden job market

If I had a chance to redo my postgrad job applications, I would focus almost exclusively on the hidden job market. At the time, I fell into the same trap that many people do and applied for as many jobs online as possible. I received interview offers for less than five percent of my job applications. It was a lonely time in my life.

I kept modifying my resumes and cover letters and applying for more and more jobs online. "Surely a resume with glittering work experience and graduate degrees from both Columbia University and Georgia

Tech should count for something," I thought. Eventually, I realized that I had to change tack and do something dramatically different.

For the most part, applying for online job postings is a big waste of time. I needed to focus on the hidden job market and its inner workings. Even after this realization, I wasn't sure what to do. I had so many questions to answer: How can I gain access to the invisible job market? How big is it? How much time should I spend on it? How long will it take to crack?

I began researching the answers to these questions and the data was surprising. Now, you might be asking, "Just how big is this invisible job market?" In her book "Quick and Quintessential Guide: Cracking the Hidden Job Market," Dr. Katharine Hansen indicates that "published estimates of the size of this market ranges from 75 to 95 percent of the total job market." According to Steven Rothberg, founder of the job search website CollegeRecruiter.com, 80 percent of jobs aren't publicly advertised.

Data on the impact of referrals on hiring rates is equally illuminating. In a revealing study conducted by CareerXRoads in 2013, it was concluded that a candidate who acquired a referral is three to four times more likely to be hired.

The invisible job market phenomenon occurs primarily because of two reasons: One is expressed by Janet Civitelli of VocationVillage.com, who contends that "hiring managers will prefer to hire someone they know, like and trust." The other reason is because of the way the job opening process works.

As illustrated in the following graphic created by J. Michael Farr of "The Very Quick Job Search," there are typically four stages of a job opening.

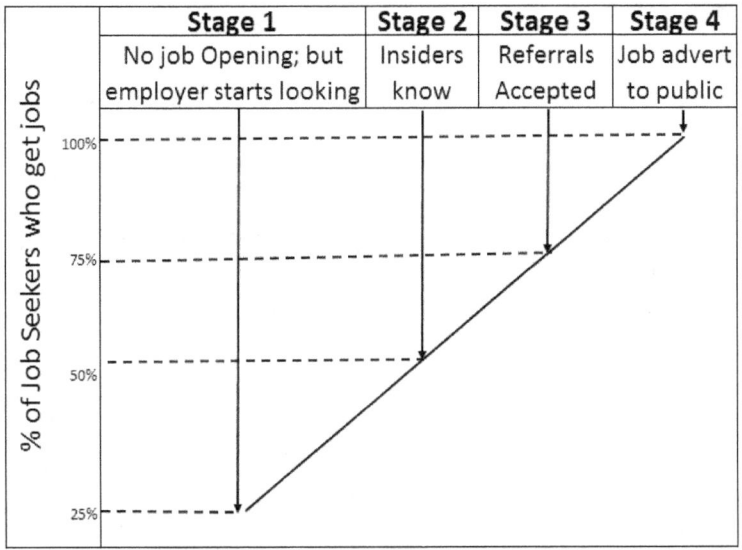

In the first stage, employers are looking for good candidates, but haven't decided exactly what they need; therefore, only about 25 percent of candidates get jobs in Stage 1.

In the second stage, it becomes obvious that they need to open job requisitions, but only a few insiders know about this; up to 50 percent of candidates are hired by Stage 2.

In the third stage, a decision has been made to advertise the job, but it would take some time yet before it's posted. During this, attempts will be made to find an internal candidate to obtain referrals for candidates through trusted networks; up to 75 percent of candidates are hired by Stage 3.

To buttress this point, TheWiseJobSearch.com stated in an article titled "Targeting Companies vs. Job Boards for Your Job Search" that "by the time an ad is actually placed, they may have multiple candidates they are already considering!"

It's clear from the foregoing analysis that the competition for a job gets fiercer and fiercer as we approach the final stages. Therefore, it's no wonder that less than 25 percent of people get jobs from postings on job boards, magazines and another media.

In spite of the arguments presented against focusing solely on online applications, it still makes sense for any job search strategy to include these applications. How much time and effort should be devoted to these? To answer this question, I suggest listening to the advice provided by Susan Adams of Forbes, who recommends that "job seekers should spend no more than 20 percent of their time answering ads (some coaches recommend only 10 percent)."

Channeling Sir Isaac Newton: How to use leverage to unlock the hidden job market

Sir Isaac Newton once said, "If I have seen further, it is by standing on the shoulders of giants." These wise words are as true today as they were in the late 1700s. Similarly, the mantra for being successful in a career should be, "If I have reached this far in my career, it is by standing on the shoulders of my giant network."

While it's common knowledge that networks are powerful, most people don't understand how they work, nor do they know how to create network effects that will propel them to greater success.

Here are some strategies to leverage networks to your benefit:

- **Understand and develop effective networks**

    Not all networks are created equal. According to Paul Ormerod in his book "Positive Linking," there are three common types of social networks: Small-World Network (SWN), Scale-Free Network (SFN), and Random Network (RN)

    - **Small-World Network (SWN):** In SWNs, many people are connected to a few contacts each. However, a few people have long distance connections (LDCs), creating an overlapping friends-of-friends structure.
    - **Scale-Free Networks (SFN):** In SFNs, many people are connected to a few contacts each and a small number of

people (called "hubs") are connected to many others.

- **Random Networks (RN):** In RNs, these networks have no discernible structure. Hubs and LDCs are not easily visible.

The key people in SWNs are the LDCs. Any strategy to network with LDCs must include broadening the scope of one's activities to include attending events outside of one's profession. A great place to find such people is through volunteer organizations.

The key strategy to be employed in SFNs is to identify and target the key connectors or hubs. Such people can be found in trade or industry associations, such as the president of the local Chamber of Commerce. Following people with large numbers of Twitter followers and selected LinkedIn influencers is also a viable strategy for SFNs.

The only way to target random networks is to meet as many people as possible. Since these networks are unstructured, they may involve a lot of work for little reward.

- **Develop a unique, personal brand**

    Andre Agassi helped popularize Canon's slogan "Image is Everything" through expensive TV ads. Thankfully, with the advent of social media, you can create a brand at a fraction of the cost of those TV ads.

What does branding have to do with the job search? More than ever before, companies are finding it difficult to tell candidates apart. The most common sales materials available to candidates – resumes and cover letters – are becoming less and less effective in a highly competitive job market. This makes creating a unique, personal brand more important than ever before.

A candidate who neglects a strong presence on Facebook, Twitter, LinkedIn and other social media sites does so at their own peril.

We recommend creating an "All Star" profile on LinkedIn. At a minimum, learn how to set up your profile, manage account settings, and add and remove contacts. We also recommend having a professional headshot photo for your profile and thoughtfully filling out the summary, experience and education sections. Additionally, we suggest taking advantage of a very powerful feature on LinkedIn known as the recommendations section. Ask people who are familiar with your work and skills to write recommendations for you. Until your profile is reasonably complete, make sure to turn off settings like "Notify Your Network?"

Another powerful way to be visible is to create your own blog on topics that you are passionate about. It's important to provide comments on blogs by target industries and key people of interest to you. Creating your own blog is a great personal branding tool.

If you decide to create one for yourself, link the blog to your profiles on the other social media websites. You should also steadily build an audience using the following approach recommended by blogging guru and author of "New Rules of Marketing and PR," David Meerman Scott:

- Create links to blog as part of email signature
- Comment on blogs and include links to your blog
- Find out what search terms people use to find you
- Update blogs on a regular basis
- Use tags to make your blogs easily searchable

Ninja tactics: How to crack the invisible job market

There are times when it's not clear at all how to reach key people who might be able to facilitate your job search or career progression. After you've exhausted your contacts on Facebook, LinkedIn and Twitter, what's left?

At this point, it may be time to pull out more stops and resort to some "ninja" strategies. Unlike the connotation associated with the name, the execution of ninja tactics in the job hunt is neither subtle nor stealthy. This approach involves direct calling (DC) of potential contacts to help you extend your network beyond the third degree connections that LinkedIn provides.

What makes it "ninja" appropriate is the method taken to gain access to key decision makers. It's all overboard, so don't worry. However, this requires underground work to find out who the right people are and where to meet them.

Recently, I met the president of a famous university in Palo Alto with whom I had unsuccessfully been trying to contact via email and LinkedIn for three months. I registered for a conference where he was scheduled to be the keynote speaker and I waited until the lunch session to talk to him and request a further meeting to discuss a proposal. I expected him to tell me to wait until the next week or later, but to my surprise he agreed to talk about my proposal that very day.

On other occasions, I have arrived an hour early to conferences, grabbed a front row seat, and made sure to ask carefully researched questions to catch the eye of a particular speaker I came to meet. This has helped me establish contacts with several high-profile CEOs and decision makers.

A much less expensive but still effective way is to "stalk" the blogs of the people you might be interested in. Get interested in their interests, be noticed by leaving comments to their posts, and establish email or Twitter correspondence. Before diving head-first into the blogosphere, make sure to answer the following questions:

- Whom do I want to reach?
- Am I passionate about this topic?
- Is the subject narrow enough?

The Steps to cracking the hidden job market

The ultimate objective of the approaches we've been exploring in this chapter is to dramatically increase your chances of landing that dream job. To conclude this chapter on how to quadruple your job success rate, we will leave you with a roadmap and some resources that can help you crack the hidden job market yourself.

Even though we will not discuss the usual strategies of LinkedIn, Facebook and Twitter here, we trust that you are already using them as part of a comprehensive strategy.

- Step 1: Target your next employer

    This can be done efficiently by using resources like Hoovers.com, Edgar-Online.com, and ReferenceUSA.com. Reference USA allows you to search through 24 million US businesses and 200,000 human resource contacts, business descriptions and links to job postings. Check with your local library for free access to this database; otherwise, individual access to information contained in it is very expensive.

- Step 2: Determine the types of jobs you might be interested in

Once you have fallen in love with a particular company, do a search on the types of positions they typically hire for and find the closest match to what you need. The idea is not to apply online for the jobs, but to tailor your resume to suit such jobs. One of the first few questions you hear when you talk to hiring managers is, "Have you checked our website for job openings?" While we now know that blindly applying online is not the way to go, make sure you've covered all your bases.

- Step 3: Identify key decision makers

In addition to using LinkedIn and your existing networks to find the key decision makers, we recommend checking out the council of business advisors (www.councilofbusinessadvisors.org), which is an association of highly experienced professionals and advisors who work primarily with business owners and executives. Members can be found by profession and specialty along with their bios and contact information (phone numbers, email addresses, websites).

An often underrated approach is to contact headhunters or recruiting agencies who tend to have a lot of information on many companies. Find a specialist agency in your target industry. You may want to review annual and 10-K reports of the target company to find some contact information.

- Step 4: Go all out

  Once you know who to contact, focus on being authentic and building relationships. Always endeavor to create low pressure encounters, such as accidental meetings at events and informational meetings (also known as "informational interviews"). It's also a good idea to spend some of your time making "cold calls" to the people you identified in Step 3. Remember, don't ask for a job, but seek advice and then you just might land your dream job.

Accessing the hidden job network is a great way to get your dream job, but this becomes even easier when you make regular networking a part of your career and part of your lifestyle. In these cases, you can come across jobs while you are not even looking.

Effective Networking

What is networking?

Networking is the process of expanding your area of influence. Your area of influence is the number of people who have a positive impression of you, the number of people who you can call on for help, or the number of people who you've been in regular contact with for the past six months. It's about building relationships with people and finding common ground.

Common misconceptions about networking

1. *You must get to know as many people as possible*
Networking is not the process of knowing or being known to as many people as possible. Just going to every event and collecting business cards

is not networking. This approach is exhaustive and ineffective. Remember, quality is much more important than quantity when it comes to networking.

2. *You must have a purpose for networking*

Networking is not done to get a certain job or to land a promotion. If you come across as trying to use the people in your network for your own gains, or if you are asking for a favor without having a strong connection, it will end up being counterproductive to your goals.

Instead, networking is done to build strong relationships in the field over a period of time. It involves keeping in touch with your contacts, helping people when they need help, and finding common ground. In the long term, if you need a business partner, job or promotion, it's easier to bring it forward to a strong network.

3. *There is a particular time and place for networking*

The concept of networking is applicable to any time and any place. Performing well and building strong relationships at your current job will help foster a strong network for future openings. A conversation with a cashier during a break can also lead to a form of networking. It's good to always look to build relationships and find common ground.

Why is networking important?

1. *You learn about events and opportunities not available to the general public*

If you have a large network of people in your field of interest, you will be among the first to hear about conferences, training events, job positions and other career opportunities. These may not always be available to the general public.

For example, a friend of mine knew that his co-worker was going to switch jobs a month before it actually happened. My friend was able to refer an acquaintance into the open position as soon as his co-worker resigned, even before the job was actually posted.

2. *You can help friends of family members if you hear of any opportunities*

If you have an active network, you can alert your personal network of any news that you hear which might be useful to them. This is a huge benefit to your network of close friends and family members.

3. *You can learn about trends in your industry*

Networking in your industry will keep you in touch with the latest trends in the industry in terms of growth rate, career paths, improvements in technology and new startups in the area.

4. *You can learn about different career paths taken by people in your current industry*

Most people at your workplace or in the industry may follow a strict career path, which is recommended by bosses and coworkers. However, some people in your network might choose a different career path that you were previously unaware of. This can open your mind to different possibilities for how your skills set can be used.

Different types of networking

1. **Events**

    Events are a vital part of networking. Be selective in the networking events you attend, especially if you have a tight schedule. Find events relevant to your interests or profession. You can find out about networking events by subscribing to a relevant, professional newsletter, joining a professional organization or through online searches. Most of the time you will learn about professional organizations through your existing network.

At every event, make sure you have business cards and are well dressed. Depending on the event, you should dress in business professional or business casual attire. Be sure to practice a 30 second speech introducing yourself before the event.

As mentioned before, quality is much more important than the quantity of your contacts. If possible, try to research network attendees and speakers beforehand so that you know whom to contact.

Introduce yourself to your contact and compliment them. Try to find common ground during your conversation. You need to spend at least 15 to 20 minutes with your contact in order to establish a strong connection by finding a strong common ground and exploring several topics of discussion. If there's a problem in his or her job or organization that you can help with, offer your services to help find a solution. At the end of your discussion, exchange business cards or phone numbers.

Follow up with your network contacts within 72 hours using the sample letters below. If anything interesting happened in your industry, follow up with your contact regarding this event via LinkedIn or text message. Discussing these interesting events is a good way to keep in touch.

2. **Informational interviews**

Informational interviews are meetings with a person in your field of interest or career with the objective of obtaining more information.

It's a great way to connect with and learn from people with decades of experience in your field.

It's also a good way to get your foot in the door at a company or for a particular position. For regular interviews, you're competing against a number of qualified candidates, but for informational interviews there is generally no interview at all. Instead, you gain knowledge about the company, industry, jobs available and company culture. You also have the opportunity to make a positive impression and discuss your qualifications. This way you're in a better position than those who just applied online for a regular interview. Informational interviews can also help you find a mentor for your career.

Use our template at the end of the chapter to contact people and get an informational interview set up.

3. Online networking

There are several resources available for online networking. The resource most commonly used for business networking is LinkedIn. Instead of spreading your time across several social networks, I recommend you focus on LinkedIn as a complement to your offline networking resources.

You can use online networking to set up informational interviews, contact headhunters and managers, or look up networking events and professional associations information.

There are several ways you can use LinkedIn for online networking:

- If you are looking for a job or just looking to learn more about a particular topic, join a LinkedIn group in your field. Use the LinkedIn search bar at the top of the page to search for groups in your field of interest and request to join the group. Once you're in the group, you have access to industry experts in your field. You can ask them direct questions and add them as contacts. You can also start a group discussion on any relevant topic. If you can do this often, you will become a well-known member of the group and potentially a well-known individual in the field.

- You can use the LinkedIn search bar for jobs in your field. You can also review the jobs or recruiters for job. LinkedIn also lets you know if anyone in your network works at the company you're interested in working for. You can then contact that person and ask them to recommend you for the job.

- You can connect with a company you are strongly interested in working for by searching for people within the company. Search results will show people in your network who can help you connect with recruiters and managers. You can also search directly for managers and senior managers and request an interview or informational interview with them.

4. **Professional association**

Professional associations are a great way to network with people in the same field of interest as you. There are professional associations for every field and most professional associations are international. They are a great resource for inside information, overall industry trends and new developments in the field. Associations Unlimited is a great tool for those looking for new associations in their field. It has a database of over 460,000 national and international associations. It is only available by subscription, so there's no point in googling it.

You can, however, access it at your local library. Most professional organizations offer reduced fees for students, so it's a great way for new career entrants to network with veterans in the field.

The biggest benefit of professional associations is the condensing of information in a world that is overloaded with information. If you are looking to learn more about your field, you can access millions of news articles, journals and books. Most professional organizations have weekly newsletters or magazines that condense the latest information in the field.

Sample Networking Letter

Dear Steve,

We met briefly at the end of our flight to Chicago two weeks ago. As I mentioned, I am changing careers from law to advertisement. You had the insight and kindness to advise me on companies that would be interested in my background.

Since our discussion, I've decided I need to get some digital advertising experience. Amazon Marketing Channel is one of the companies I'm interested, and I noticed you have a connection to their marketing manager Rick Smith. Would you be able to introduce us or pass along a recommendation for me to him?

Sincerely,

(Your name here)

(Reference: Ref: http://idealistcareers.org/13-helpful-email-templates-to-use-while-job-searching/)

Sample Informational Interview Request

Subject: Informational Interview Request from Georgia Tech Student

Dear Ms. (insert name here),

Sam Hoffmayer, Assistant Dean of Georgia Tech, suggested I contact you and asked me to pass along his regards. I understand you have expertise in solar cell technology and I'm very interested in learning more about your work at Solar City. I wish to pursue a career in solar engineering upon graduation from my university next year.

Over the past two years, I've worked for the Solar Jackets team, which builds solar powered cars and modifies existing cars to allow for solar utilization. This sparked my interest in solar cell research.

I plan to move to California after graduation and would greatly appreciate the opportunity to meet with you to discuss your projects as well as career opportunities available in the field.

I realize you are a busy person, but I would appreciate your time. I will be leaving for summer break on May 25 and it would be great to meet you before then, if your schedule permits. I will give you a call next week to check on the possibility of setting up a meeting.

Thank you in advance for your help.

Sincerely,

(Your name/signature here)

(Your email)

(Your address)

(Your phone number)

Sample Thank You Letter

Dear Mrs. Short,

Thank you very much for taking the time to talk to me. I found your advice very useful and will use it to obtain an internship at CapGemini Consulting.

As you suggested, I called their senior manager Tim Starr and will be meeting with one of her consultants next week.

I hope you enjoy the rest of your time in Austria before moving back to Chicago. I look forward to talking to you when you return. Thank you for your help and I will keep you posted on my job search progress.

Sincerely,

(Your Name Here)

(Email)

(Phone number)

(Reference: http://hls.harvard.edu/dept/opia/job-search-toolkit/networking-tips/sample-networking-emails-and-thank-you-notes/)

At this point, you have done the very important task of getting important job leads that can get you your next job. However, it is also important to apply online to jobs that interest you. Your leads might tell you sometimes to apply online or you might also come across a job online that seems like a dream fit.

Resume, Cover Letters and Job Applications

A Good First Impression: How to get your resume noticed

Have you ever wondered why you never get called for interviews? It's most frustrating when the job description is exactly the same as the job you've held for a long time – yet you don't get the call.

A well-known sage once said, "There is no second chance to make a good first impression." Much the same, your resume is an opportunity for you to get noticed. It's the icebreaker that colors a conversation. If a hiring manager can't get a clear sense of who you are and how you can get the boss off his or her back within 20 seconds, you're out of luck.

In this chapter, we'll review the most common reasons why prospective applicants don't get called for interviews. We'll also provide you with tips for designing a resume that will get you noticed.

Tailor your resume to each job

One of the most common habits of many job seekers is to apply to as many jobs as possible—my friends and I compare this behavior to the dating game. The logic behind this is that if you apply for 100 jobs, you'll get called for at least 10 interviews. In reality, though, you're lucky to get called for five at most.

What's the problem? One of the main reasons is the lack of a tailored resume for the job in which they're applying for.

As a rule of thumb, I recommend spending up to four hours customizing your resume and cover letter for each job. Carefully review keywords in the job posting and try to use as many of them as are relevant to your qualifications. You have to imagine yourself as the hiring manager – would you hire yourself if you reviewed your own resume?

One useful tool for cross-checking how well your resume matches the job description is using the website www.jobscan.co. Before sending your resume, paste it and the corresponding job description on Jobscan to see how your resume stacks up.

This tool allows you to effectively determine the following:

- Match rate: See how well your resume matches up with the job description. The website rates your match on a scale of 0 to 100 percent.
- Skills: See how your hard and soft skills listed on your resume compare with those in the job description.
- Keywords: Compare one-word terms listed in the job description to the ones mentioned in your resume.
- Find jobs with similar skills: The results page provides a list of jobs with similar skills to those found in the job description. Search results are usually within a 25-mile radius of your

computer's IP address; however, this feature may not work in some locations.

Jobscan is very simple to use. Follow these easy steps to measure the quality of your resume:

Step 1: Visit www.jobscan.co and sign up for an account.

Step 2: Choose a plan. There are currently three plans. The free version allows you to do up to five comparisons. There are two options to pay for full features. The most popular is one that gives a whole month of unlimited comparisons for free.

Step 3: Copy and paste your job description and resume, click scan and wait for your results. It's that easy!

Jobscan is a tool that gives job seekers an instant analysis of how well their resumes are tailored for specific jobs. Likewise, it shows how resumes can be better optimized for an applicant tracking system (ATS).

Remember, your resume is not a laundry list

When you're out shopping, you've probably got a list of things you need to get. Having a laundry list can help save money and makes trips to the market efficient and less stressful. However, as handy as these lists can be, they're useless when it comes to the job hunt.

If your resume reads like a laundry list of things you've done in the past, it leaves a lot of room for interpretation. A majority of resume reviewers are busy with their own day-to-day jobs and duties, so they won't have time to interpret the extent of your skills and abilities.

It's tempting to fall in love with your vast work experience and to try to include as much of it as you can on your resume. You should be proud of your accomplishments! But you must stop and think! Your work experience may be impressive, but so is that of the competition.

Instead of falling into the tempting habit of listing your impressive library of experiences, think about what the hiring manager is looking for and carefully select the experiences that match with what is required.

Make your resume ATS-friendly

"By the way, what is an ATS?" a friend wondered aloud as the presenter of our resume writing class at Nova Job Center droned on using acronyms that nobody understood.

ATS stands for Applicant Tracking System. It's a software used by most companies to screen resumes. Unfortunately, most standard resumes are formatted in such a way that they cannot be properly read by the ATS.

Before you submit a resume online, make sure it's in a format that can be accurately read by the ATS. Later in this chapter, we'll explore best practices for creating an ATS-friendly resume.

Always include a cover letter

I find it incredibly disheartening when a candidate, usually in a hurry to move on to the next job application, declines to submit a cover letter for a job. Doing this is like going into battle and leaving one of your best weapons at home. It's a colossal mistake! How else can you highlight in detail your most impressive accomplishments? As a rule of thumb, always include a cover letter with your job applications, whether it's required or not. We have great tips on cover letter creation at the end of the chapter.

Find an internal champion

Even though you shouldn't forget all the tips mentioned above, the best way to get your resume positively reviewed is having a personal connection to the hiring managers.

In many cases, the difference between getting your resume reviewed or not is simply based on whether you know someone close to the hiring manager. I like to call these people "internal champions."

These are people who, other than yourself, have an interest in having you hired. Such a champion can be a friend with close ties to the hiring manager who also values your relationship, an employee who could get a referral bonus, or a headhunter who is paid a commission if you are hired.

Before you submit your resume, do the required due diligence and find out who can send your resume to the hiring manager directly. Find out as much as you can about the company, its hiring manager, and the recruiters for the position, then use what you've found to support your social networks (LinkedIn, Facebook, Twitter, alumni, etc.).

Follow up regularly (once every two weeks) with your internal champion if you haven't heard back for a while.

Getting Past the ATS Robots: How to increase your chances of an interview

A few years ago, I learned one of the most important lessons of my life when I was rejected by a 200-pound bouncer at a trendy nightclub in Puebla, Mexico. As a single man, it felt really chastening to have my dreams of meeting beautiful women shattered at the gate. What are a person's chances if they can't even get through the door? I later figured out that I didn't meet the dress code.

Sadly, job seekers are often in a similar position and don't get invited to the interview (or dance, in my case) because of rejections by an invisible, digital bouncer named "ATS." The Applicant Tracking System is a recruiting software that, among other things, is used to screen and rank candidates.

Unfortunately, it's not always able to properly read resumes submitted online because they haven't been "dressed up" or formatted properly. As a result, many resumes are rejected at the gate and never meet a human eye. Most HR departments use ATS software to sort through the overwhelming number of resumes received online.

We will spend time identifying the most common reasons for resume failure (RFRF) and rejection by the ATS as well as review practical tips to help make your resume ATS friendly.

RFRF1: ATS doesn't appreciate style

The ATS has poor taste when it comes to resume "fashion." Therefore, the stylistic additions that would usually make a resume standout to a human reviewer will unfortunately work against you.

A key tip to making your resume ATS friendly is to avoid graphics, layouts and exotic fonts. As a rule of thumb, the barer bones the resume is (stylistically speaking), the easier it will be for the ATS. Think simple, plain text document rather than a PowerPoint document. Use common fonts, such as Times New Roman and Ariel instead of the fancier Corsiva or Syncopate.

RFRF2: Resume format is not compatible with ATS

Many ATS systems misread resumes in the PDF and HTML format and as a result will discard them.

Always use Microsoft Word. Avoid saving your resume in HTML or PDF formats, because text cannot always be properly extracted from PDF documents. It's best to use Microsoft Word or to save your resume as a plain text document instead.

RFRF3: ATS cannot read tables, fields, headers and footers in Microsoft Word

Tables, fields and footers keep information organized and tidy to the human eye. However, they get scrambled and become unreadable by many ATS systems. For example, data in the leftmost column of a table may appear at the top of a converted resume or could even become scrambled, and page numbers may show up in the middle of the page.

This doesn't mean your resume can't look somewhat presentable. When it comes to formatting, use tabs instead of tables or columns and capitalization instead of common header terms and consistent fonts. Always start resume sections with capitalized terms and put them on separate lines. For example, you should put the various sections (such as job objective, work experience and education) on separate lines, as shown below:

JOB OBJECTIVE

WORK EXPERIENCE

EDUCATION

It's smart to put your contact information at the beginning of your resume in an unformatted fashion, like this:

John Doe

1200 Harker Avenue

Palo Alto, CA 94301

John.Doe@jobsgalore.net

To conclude, here are three best practices and resources to help get your resume past the ATS and land that coveted interview:

- Customize each resume with targeted keywords to match the job description
- Always have two versions of each resume: one for online submissions and another to respond to email requests

- Use resources available at www.jobscan.co and www.sovren.com. Input your resume to ensure that it's ATS friendly.

Anatomy of the cover letter: How to craft a job-winning cover letter

The cover letter is your opportunity to highlight in detail your best accomplishments and prove why you're the best person for the job. The goal is to stimulate the interest of the reviewer and convince them to call you for an interview. It's your personal sales pitch and should be well thought and honest. To write a great cover letter, start out by thinking about the prospective employer's needs and how you can prove that you're the best fit for the role.

In this chapter, we'll review best practices and tips for writing a cover letter that will get you noticed and give you a leg up on the competition. We'll explore six key aspects of a cover letter and look at some examples.

Components of a cover letter

- The Salutation: Always address your cover letter to a specific person. Make sure you know the name of the person likely to read your cover letter.

    Dear Dr. Adams...

- The Hook: This is where you provide the reviewer a reason to continue reading.

Remember, they don't have more than a few seconds, so keep it succinct.

I learned from a recent job posting on campus that you are looking for an experienced sales manager to lead ABC Company into new markets. I would like to talk with you about how my 10 years of experience implementing successful sales strategies in emerging markets can help you achieve your goal.

- The Pitch: To position yourself to be called for an interview, you must make a convincing case in as few words as possible. Explain to your prospective employer why you're the best person for the job.

I have repeatedly outperformed in the face of start-up, turnaround and growth challenges. I have done this in diverse markets and tough economic conditions, generating hundreds of millions of dollars in sales. I have developed a rare combination of experience, vision and leadership – and that's exactly the combination your company needs to achieve its full potential.

(Courtesy "Guerilla Marketing for Job Hunters 3.0")

- The Brag: Now that you've hooked them, keep their interest going by highlighting your best accomplishments and showing what makes you stand out. It's important to make sure that these examples are relevant to the position you're applying for. To maximize the impact of your accomplishments, frame them using the STAR framework (Situation, Task, Action, Result). I recommend highlighting three to five of your best accomplishments.)

As the global sales manager for XYZ, I was tasked with increasing the disappointing sales of the company's new product line in Peru and Tanzania. I recruited a local sales team and spent six months conducting an in-depth market analysis. This resulted in an increase in market share from five to 25 percent.

As project manager at the City of San Jose capital Improvement Program, I was tasked with managing a project that was under budget and six months behind schedule. I held several negotiation sessions with stakeholders to streamline the budget and schedule. This resulted in 50 percent savings in the budget and the project was completed two weeks ahead of time.

- The Next Step: To conclude your cover letter, ask for a quick call to talk about the position. The key here is to provide a time slot that you are available. Ask them to suggest a couple of times they might be available if your time slot is not convenient.

- Contact Information: Do not neglect to provide information on how they might contact you. This should preferably include your email, LinkedIn profile, personal website and phone number.

Akash Renato

www.akash.net

akash@akash.net

www.linkedin.com/in/Akash

7186648732

Once you've successfully mastered the art of drafting resumes and cover letters that can capture the attention of HR personnel and hiring managers, you can expect the calls for interviews to start pouring in. When that happens, congratulations! You're one step closer to receiving the job of your dreams!

Ace the Interview

Make a point to attend every interview you are invited to. Interviewing is like playing sports – practice makes perfect. To shorten your learning curve and make your life easier, here are tips from our founding team who have been through hundreds of interviews.

Different Types of Interviews

There are dozens of different ways people are interviewed based on the competition for the jobs, hiring timeline, job type, company size, etc. Some of the most common interview types include:

HR Screening Interview

In most companies, HR personnel screen the candidate through a quick 15 to 20-minute discussion. They will generally ask you about your career goals, your interest in the company and your compensation requirements. By doing this, they gauge your level of interest and future career expectations.

For students, these types of interviews are usually conducted as talks at career fairs and company information sessions. For those already in the work force, HR generally calls them after looking at their profile and experience.

Phone Interview with Hiring Manager

After the first HR interview, there is often another phone call with the hiring manager that lasts between 30 minutes to one hour. The hiring manager tries to understand the skillset and interest of the candidate and whether or not he or she is a good fit for the position and company.

There is no set rule for this type of interview. It could be a set of behavioral questions, technical questions, or a combination of both. A behavioral interview question is one in which the candidate is asked questions about his reaction to different work situations. A technical interview questions the knowledge level of the candidate.

In cases where the candidate is local, the company may skip the phone interview and call the student in for a site interview.

Final Round Interview at Site with Different Hiring Managers

Once the candidate passes the phone interview, he (or she) is invited on site where he will be interviewed by several hiring managers as well as some senior members of the team. He is asked a series of behavioral and technical questions by each interviewer. The interviewers will then discuss each candidate in detail before making the final hiring decision.

Questions asked during this interview vary, depending on the company. Larger companies or MNCs have standardized interview structures with mostly behavioral questions. Managers take notes on the details of the candidate's interest, technical ability and answer.

In smaller companies or startups, interviews typically follow a casual conversation format. Managers are interested in how a candidate would be able to interact with a small team as well as his technical skills. It's extremely important for them to know that potential candidates would get along well with the team that is critical to the growth of the organization. In larger organizations, bad employers can be transferred to another parts of the organization for a better fit.

For highly technical positions, candidates may have a written portion of the interview set with technical or problem solving questions. Some of the questions do not have defined answers, but employers are interested in how they arrived at their answer. Managers want to know a candidate's ability to solve a variety of problems, not necessarily whether they know the right answer.

STAR Interview Format

Almost every interview has a portion that is dedicated to behavioral questions that reveal how candidates behave in different situations. These questions might include things like, "How did you react when faced with a difficult coworker?" or "Describe how you react when faced with a difficult situation." These questions are best answered in a Situation, Task, Action, Result (STAR) format.

For example, let's say you're asked, "How did you handle a situation where you made a mistake?" Here's how to answer following the STAR format:

> **Situation (S):** Once I made a mistake when I manually entered the wrong quote

for one of the suppliers for the product. This resulted in a higher price for the product by 15 percent than I computed. The product had to be sent for review because it was priced higher than the competition.

Task (T): I realized the mistake three days later as I was creating a system that automatically linked the supplier database with my worksheet. I notified my manager of the mistake and recomputed the quote.

Action (A): I also showed my manager and team the new system I created, which would prevent further mistakes from happening.

Result (R): The product was sent into the market since it was cheaper and better than the competition. The system linking the supplier database to ours was set as a standard for the company and was able to prevent further mistakes by both myself and my coworkers. All previous quotes done by others was rechecked with this software and several other mistakes were corrected, saving the company money.

Put together, this is a good answer to give during a behavioral interview. It describes the situation in detail, highlighting your technical ability and your integrity.

It's suggested to have a list of five answers to interview questions that double as behavioral questions. Here are some of the most common behavioral interview questions:

- Describe a situation where you had to deal with a difficult coworker
- Describe a situation where you had to overcome a difficult challenge
- Describe a situation where you had to work under pressure
- Describe a situation in which you worked with a team
- Describe a decision you made that wasn't popular and how you handled it
- Describe a situation in which you disagreed with your boss

- Describe a situation in which you had to motivate your coworkers

Make sure you have answers to these common behavioral questions and keep building on these as you continue to get more interviews.

Interview Template: Your 30-minute interview preparation template

For any interview, there's a list of items you must complete in terms of company research, job fit and questions for the company. All of these are listed in the Interview Preparation template in Appendices and also in the link below. It should be completed in no more than 30 minutes. The template encompasses everything you need to prepare for in terms of company research and how well you fit with the company.

The templates are included in Appendix 1 (Interview Template -Empty) and Appendix 2 (Sample Interview Template – Filled) at the end of the book.

Preparation for Technical Questions

Technical questions will usually come up in interviews if you are changing jobs. The employer is looking to see how much you know about a particular subject area. Here are a few tips to overcome the technical portion:

- Be honest with your knowledge about a subject. They can test you out with a few questions on any subject that you claim to be knowledgeable about. A lot of these questions test your practical knowledge and can only be answered if you have worked in the field.

- Be honest with what you need to learn on the job. The company is willing to train you on some portions of the job if you bring significant transferrable skills to the table.

- If you have transferrable skills, describe them in detail every chance you get. Use the STAR format and bring work samples in your portfolio.

Dress Appropriately

Most interviews call for business professional or business casual attire. Business casual is usually for plant and factory environments. If you're in doubt, dress business professional to be safe. Make sure your clothes fit your body well. Get a tailor made suit if you can afford it.

Go get 'em

Even after you've prepared well and dressed for the occasion, you could still be extremely nervous about actually landing your dream job. Before going into any interview, you have to get in the right mental state and remember that even if this interview is a failure, it's practice and there will be plenty more. This thought process will help ease the nerves.

Just like everything else, you will get better at interviewing the more you do it. If you have limited experience interviewing, the best practice is to try and do as many as you can. Once you master interviewing, you will never need to worry about landing a job.

Choosing Between Jobs

Congratulations! At this point, you've mastered the interview process and have your choice of jobs. Many people wish they were in the same position as you, they wish they had the same problem. However, keep in mind that the job you choose is critical and you have an important decision to make. This choice will dictate your life for the next few years if you wish to maintain a stable job history.

In this chapter, we will list out a few factors you should consider while deciding which job is right for you. We break them down into controllable and uncontrollable factors.

Controllable Factors

These are factors you can determine through research and you can use some of the techniques in this book to get the information you need. Rate each of these factors on a scale of zero to five. Five indicates that it matches your expectations completely and zero indicates that it does not at all.

1. Career Relevance

If you researched the industry and the position in Chapter 1 before you started applying for jobs, you should be landing jobs that you are interested in. This should be a "4" or "5." However, if you already had jobs lined up before you got this book, this will require a little extra thought.

2. **Growth Potential**

This indicates the possibility for growth in salary or position throughout your career. You can determine this by talking to other people who have started off in the same position. Complete a LinkedIn search for professionals who have worked in the same position in the same company. Have a look at their career path. Does it match your expectations?

3. **Location**

This is a very subjective field, but is of great importance to a lot of people. Do you have to live close to your family? Is this position in the city or the countryside? Are most similar jobs in the city or countryside? Are you a city or country person? Is the weather something you would like? When rating this, see if the current position matches your expectations. Consider potential jobs you might be interested in the future that are also in a similar location.

4. Salary

This is of utmost importance to a lot of people. Everyone wants to get paid as much as possible to get that great vacation to Hawaii, or to increase their savings, or to pay for their child's education. However, it's important to realize that every job has a range of values that are paid to an employee based on his/her relevant experience, job location and education. This range is listed on websites like Payscale or Salary. You can try to negotiate salaries to the upper range. Check out some of the great tips in Chapter 9 on how to best do this. You must also realize that you might have to undergo a pay cut if you switch fields or industries without any significant transferrable skills.

Uncontrollable Factors

The uncontrollable factors are factors that cannot be accounted for in company or field research. The workplace is a chaotic place and every job, every person, every manager can have an impact to your happiness on the job. There is no way of finding out unless you talk to people who are working in the same team. If you can, try to get their contact information on LinkedIn and give them a call. Be aware that they might not be entirely truthful as they are working for the team that they are talking about. It's your call.

1. **Management**

There are all kinds of bosses in the world and every boss has their strengths and weaknesses. However, there are bosses that are hated by everyone they come across. These bosses can make a great job miserable. If you hear about this kind of boss beforehand, beware!

2. **Team Environment**

Different personalities prosper in different environments. Some people are stimulated by environments that are challenging and active while others are intimidated by this kind of environment. Some people like a laid back environment while others are bored to death by this kind of environment.

3. **Creativity**

Does your job involve using your creativity to solve problems on a daily basis? Or is it doing the same task in a repetitious manner? Which do you prefer?

4. **Work/Life Balance**

This factor generally depends on your industry. Certain industries have longer hours than others. In some cases, however, the hours can change depending on the team environment and manager.

What's Important to You?

All these factors are important; some of them are more important to you than others. Others might view these factors differently. For example, a single guy starting his career would give more importance to factors like career relevance and growth potential while a married person with three kids might give higher priority to Work/Life Balance and location. Rate each factor on a scale of 0 to 5 based on how important they are to you. A rating of "5" indicates that the factor is of utmost importance to you while a rating of "1" indicates that you do not care about it.

Job Selection Matrix

Great! At this point, you have done enough groundwork to make an informed decision. If you are not able to get all the information for the uncontrollable factors, don't worry about it. You have done all that you can. The matrix below aggregates all the factors for both jobs and lets you decide.

Factor Name	Importance	Job A Factor Value	Job B Factor Value	Job A Total	Job B Total
Career Relevance					
Growth Potential					
Location					
Salary					
Management					
Team Environment					
Creativity					
Work/Life Balance					
Total					

Let's take the example of Bob from previous chapters. He has followed all the advice in this book and has landed two great jobs. Let's call them Job A and Job B. He goes through the job selection matrix process for each job and comes up with a score.

In the second column, Bob determines how important each of the factors are. For example, Career Relevance and Growth Potential are most important for him so he gives them each a value of "5."

In the third column, Bob thinks about the extent to which Job A satisfies each factor. For example, Job A's salary is low, so he gives it a value of "2" while the growth potential is high, so he gives it "4." Bob then does the same for Job B in Column 4.

He then multiplies the values in Column 2 and 3 and puts the product in Column 5. He multiplies Column 2 and 4 and puts the product in Column 6.

He then adds all the values in Column 5 (Job A Totals) to get a Master Total of 91. He does the same for Column 6 (Job B totals) to get a master total of 71. This indicates to Bob that Job A is 20 points better than Job B (or 28% better). Bob chooses Job A.

Factor Name	Importance	Job A Factor Value	Job B Factor Value	Job A Total	Job B Total
Career Relevance	5	4	3	20	15
Growth Potential	5	4	4	20	20
Location	4	4	2	16	8
Salary	3	2	4	6	12
Management	4	N/A	N/A	-	-
Team Environment	4	N/A	N/A	-	-
Creativity	4	4	2	16	8
Work/Life Balance	4	3	2	12	8
Master Total				**91(Job A is better)**	71

Bob chooses Job A based on what's important to him in his job search criteria. It is customized to his satisfaction and he chooses a job with more career relevance and growth potential even though it pays him less. Someone else might have picked Job B if he considered salary as very important to his career.

Now that you have figured out where you want to work you can start negotiating your final salary with your employer.

Negotiate the Final Deal

Before You Start: Seek to Understand the What and the Why

Two prominent chefs are hard-pressed for time and are fighting over the last orange left in the kitchen. They both need it to finalize their recipes for the president's dinner. After minutes of haggling they reach a compromise and split the orange in half and rush to finish their dishes.

One chef squeezes the juice from his half orange and pours it into the special sauce he is making, but the juice wasn't enough for his recipe. The other grates the peel from the other half of the orange and stirs the scrapings into the batter for his cake, but he too didn't have enough peels for his cake.

The irony is that one chef only needed the peels and the other only needed the juice. The obvious mistake both chefs made was they focused on each other's position (the what) and not each other's interests (the why). Both chefs would have been better off if they had peeled the orange and taken the parts they needed.

The above story illustrates the importance of seeking to understand one's own positions and interests as well as that of the other party.

Gather Relevant Information: Knowledge is Power

It is imperative to learn as much as possible about the person or company you are negotiating with.

Understand their motivations, limitations, positions, interests and priorities. Search Google, social media and other publicly available sources of information as part of your research. Within reason, reach out to people close to the negotiating party and learn as much as you can. Information gathering is not limited to learning about the counterparty. It is equally important to understand your own motivations, positions, interests and priorities before beginning any negotiation.

Some information to gather before entering a negotiation includes:

- Who are the competitors to the company?
- What is the typical salary range for similar jobs?
- How much are people in similar roles making at the company?

- How well is the company doing?
- Who is the hiring manager?
- How many people are applying for the same position?
- Is there flexibility for negotiating a salary? If not, can bonuses or other perks such as vacation or work from home be negotiated?

Understand the Constraints

The very nature of a negotiation implies the existence of constraints. It is absolutely important to establish for yourself the minimum you would accept in a negotiation. It is equally important to understand what the other party is willing to offer or accept. This is called the reservation point. It is the point beyond which a party will not go. We will use the purchase of a house to illustrate this point.

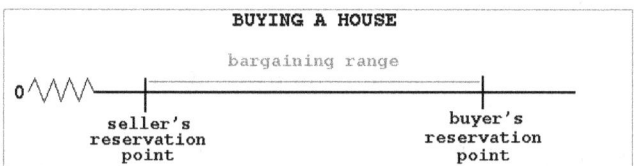

The reservation points in a real estate transaction for a seller is the minimum price at which they would sell a house. For the buyer it is the maximum amount of money they are willing to pay for the house. The bargaining range is the distance between the two reservation points. It is also called the Zone of Possible Agreement.

Another potentially limiting factor in a negotiation is whether or not one is negotiating from a position of strength. Usually the person with the most time, money or options has greater leverage and may not have the incentive to compromise. For example, if you are desperate for a job you will probably not have much leverage when it comes to a salary negotiation. To counteract this, make sure you find alternatives in preparation for the real possibility that you may have to walk away. Also make sure that you understand what you bring to the table and your own constraints. I recommend creating an inventory of your best qualities and constraints so that you do not sell yourself short or ask for a pie in the sky.

Build Relationships

A recurring theme we observe in our everyday experiences is that good relationships are a fundamental requirement for a successful life. People will walk through fire to make things happen for you if they trust and like you. The deeper the relationship, the greater the probability of success in almost any endeavor, including negotiations.

We advise playing the long game when it comes to negotiations. As much as possible, take time to cultivate relationships with the other party. Pay into a charity or support a cause they cherish, help them organize a volunteer event, or comment on their blog posts.

Optimal Salary Negotiation Tactics

A question we get asked a lot is, "What are the best tactics to use during a salary negotiation?" We invite you to come along for the ride to discover some key negotiation tactics. This chapter is based in part on insightful studies on negotiations at MIT. For a more in-depth look at this and other topics please visit MIT Negotiation Basics.

Step 1: Write down your interests and reservation points (the minimum salary and conditions you are willing to accept). Things could change so revisit these points as you gather more information or your situation changes.

For example, if you are seeking a salary of $130,000 and are absolutely determined not to accept a salary less than $100,000, a life situation or circumstance could force your hand one way or the other. On a positive note, you could come up with a business idea and decide that you are no longer available on the job market and will go make millions for yourself; on the other hand, a medical emergency could cause you to accept a lower salary than your preferred minimum.

I strongly suggest doing a pre-mortem and imagining what could go wrong or what your options are if you don't get the job. Always think about a Plan B in advance.

Step 2: Research the interests and reservation point of the employer. The reservation point for the employer is the maximum they are willing or able to pay. A good starting point is to use online resources such as Glassdoor.com, Payscale.com or Salary.com to find out the range of salaries offered for similar positions and locations. In some cases, an employer cannot offer a salary beyond the range posted. In all cases, remember that the salary is not the only thing you can negotiate. Complete your research on vacation, bonuses and other benefits and keep these in mind.

Step 3: Ask for an amount as close to the reservation point of the employer as possible (preferably a range with one amount that is two percent lower than the employer's maximum and 10% higher than it). This is especially true if you have all the relevant qualifications for the job and leverage. For maximum leverage, I recommend having more than one job offer at hand and starting your job search before you need actually need to. It's no fun having to find a job while struggling to pay the rent and other bills.

Knowing who the company's competitors are or what the market pays for the position is supercritical. However, it is important not to get hung up on the salary alone. In some cases, it is possible to negotiate items like longer vacations, student loan assistance, scheduling and more.

Step 4: Seek a settlement as close to the reservation point of the employer as possible. However, be willing to move your own reservation point if circumstances dictate that. For instance, the salary may be less than what you want but the job itself may open the door to much greater opportunities.

Step 5: Seek a win-win situation by doing your best to ensure both you and the employer are satisfied with the outcome. This may not happen right away, so try to keep your employer's interests and constraints in mind.

Step 6: In a perfect world, you would get everything you ask for and happily go on with your life. Unfortunately, reality requires some give and take in negotiations. See the big picture and be willing to compromise within reason. In cases where a compromise cannot be reached, be willing and ready to walk away.

Keep in mind the incredibly powerful lyrics from Kenny Rogers famous song the gambler:

"You've got to know when to hold 'em

Know when to fold 'em

Know when to walk away

And know when to run"

Mastering Your Job

Key Insights for Job Mastery

"It is not that we have so little time but that we lose so much. ... The life we receive is not short but we make it so; we are not ill provided but use what we have wastefully"

Seneca

Reading Seneca's words makes us think about how we could make better use of the short lives we've been given. The questions that came to mind were:

Can one achieve mastery if their job is boring?

How can one discover what their life's calling is?

How can a person with no obvious talent make a significant impact?

These questions are particularly important for person taking on a new role. Even for people who spend their adult lives working jobs they don't particularly enjoy, it's important to be great at something. At the very least, this could help provide a sense of meaning and pride.

The best work we've found on the subject of mastery are by bestselling authors Robert Green and Angela Duckworth. We can lean on their insights and decades of research to provide tips on how to attain mastery and extraordinary success in any endeavor.

Insights for Mastery

Effort is much more important than natural talent

Greene asserts there is no natural link between inborn talent and mastery. A common finding throughout decades of research is that talent doesn't always lead to significant achievement. This is no surprise according to William James, because most people use so little of their abilities that talent is not as important as it might seem on the surface. To further buttress this point, extensive research by Angela Duckworth in her book "Grit" indicates that passion, hard work and perseverance are much greater predictors of success than talent alone. According to Duckworth's model for performance, effort carries more than twice the weight of talent.

SKILL = TALENT x EFFORT

PERFORMANCE = SKILL x EFFORT

In other words:

PERFORMANCE = TALENT x EFFORT^2

Cultivate a learning attitude

More than talent, one of the key predictors of mastery is interest. This requires the enjoyment of learning for learning's sake. People with passion don't default to seeking higher positions, roles or money. A learning attitude that is fueled by interest and curiosity opens the mind up to incredible opportunities for growth and may lead to the discovery of a true passion or life's calling.

Look for any and every opportunity to understand why things are the way they are, learn how they work, and find ways of making improvements.

Find a mentor

This is an important "shortcut" because learning things on your own can be a very hard and unnecessary expenditure of energy and resources. Find a mentor who can help you reach your goals; this will speed up the time it takes to see results and enhance the quality of the results.

A good mentor will help you find your own way, even if you eventually surpass him/her. Working with a mentor provides a kind of apprenticeship that has helped propel greats like Beethoven and Mozart.

Understand the system

Being an apprentice is an important first step for learning. However, you need to improve to a point where you can place your own mark on things.

Once you understand the why's of things, be willing to challenge convention and get things done. Question everything, even things that are considered sacred. Even if nothing comes of it, you will be a better person for it. Remember to evaluate both sides of each issue from the perspective of the proponents and detractors.

Be open minded, fearless and willing to offend. Robert Greene urges you to be bold, think in unconventional ways and be willing to be ridiculed for your ideas...some of them might just change the world

Go the extra mile

Go out of your way to do things that may not show any tangible short-term rewards. Volunteer for things at work that are not within your job description and see a world of opportunities open up to you. Going the extra mile also allows you to discover interests that you never knew you had and can open the door to your life's calling.

Seek further training

To reach new heights, it's critical to prepare yourself with further training. As Isaac Newton said, "If I have seen this far, it is by standing on the shoulders of giants."

Training will provide you with a deeper understanding of your work that will allow you to be innovative. Getting further training through certifications with professional bodies or through coursework from resources such as Coursera also gives credibility and makes it easier for others to accept your ideas.

Practice and more practice

Quantity and quality of practice is what separates the truly great from the rest of us.

According to one study, to truly master an art it takes approximately 10,000 hours of practice.

Practice allows you to develop an automatic connection between things that may seem unrelated in the subconscious.

Be gritty

Grit is a combination of interest, passion and perseverance. To be gritty means to seek to accomplish feats harder than what you can comfortably achieve and soldiering on in spite of the inevitable failures along the way.

Why are we so afraid of failure? According to Nietzsche, "That which does not kill us, makes us stronger." We don't recommend taking the statement literally, but we can agree that to grow in any endeavor one must take on and overcome many challenges. One must be willing to embrace failure as part of the growth process.

While we subscribe to the idea of thinking and dreaming big, life's experience has taught us that it's better to start with goals that are achievable as well as a reasonable amount of difficulty instead of shooting for the stars right away.

For example, if your goal is to improve your endurance from a one-minute plank to a 30-minute plank, it would make sense to aim for an attainable target of one and half minutes in the first week instead of shooting for 10 minutes and falling flat on your face. Don't be afraid to fail but you can prevent failures by starting with realistic goals. Catastrophic failures can completely discourage you and prevent you from attaining goals that you would otherwise have achieved with careful planning.

The risk of aiming high is that you might not achieve what you seek at first. Therefore, it's important to accept failure as an integral part of the mastery process. It's said that Thomas Edison succeeded with his lightbulb invention after almost 10,000 failed experiments. Just like Edison, train yourself to become a paragon of grit.

Diversify your interests

"An ecosystem that has the maximum amount of diversity is the richest," said Robert Greene. Just as in nature and in business, a diversified portfolio minimizes risk and can provide the highest returns. Strengthen your chances of success by understanding how other areas impact what you do. A good understanding of a broad range of activities will allow you to make a bigger contribution and provide a basis for innovation.

Seek regular feedback

Like most people, you might be terrified of any feedback that is critical. Feedback, if properly solicited and received, can serve as a great tool for improvement.

Having said that, you need to develop an internal compass that allows you to be the final arbiter on all feedback relating to your work. Even people with the best intentions can kill your dreams without meaning to. A review of the biographies of great men should make us wary of feedback, especially from experts. Beethoven, Charles Dickens and Benjamin Franklin are a few examples of people who were told they would never be good at their crafts. Thank God they did not give up on the basis of the feedback from so called "experts."

Here is the summary of the steps we recommend taking before you start your new job.

Step 1: Before you Start – Prepare your mind

Refresh your mind by taking a mini vacation. Read some enlightening books. We recommend "Mastery" by Robert Green and "Grit" by Angela Duckworth.

Write down the core requirements of the new role. Match the skills required with skills you already possess and highlight areas that you need to work on. Find out ways to beef up any skills you may need on the job before starting.

Step 2: The First Week – Meet and greet and take care of the paperwork

Meet with your supervisor or management team to discuss the first set of priorities and overall vision for the role. Get any paperwork and early orientation requirements out of the way.

Set up one-on-one meetings with as many of the people you'll be working with as possible and ask them about what they do.

Pay attention to areas of your new job and the company you are most interested in. In particular, things that align with your interests. This list can be updated on a monthly basis.

Step 3: First Quarter on the Job – Seek to be mentored

Find a mentor(s).

Spend time cultivating the relationship and seek to meet at least once a month. Remember that a mentoring relationship takes time to develop and the more informal the better.

It may make sense to have multiple mentors depending on your situation. However, we don't recommend more than two mentors at a time.

Step 4: First year

Attend internal and external training events and conferences.

Complete any required certifications.

Join at least one professional or industry group.

Make at least one presentation to the board, host a conference or co-author a paper.

Consider starting an office blog or organizing a service event or potluck.

Ask for feedback from your supervisor and coworkers.

Conclusion

Hopefully by now you have completed your ATS-friendly resumes and cover letters, mastered the hidden job market, completed many successful interviews, negotiated a great salary and bonus package, and you're now ready to start your job. We have enjoyed taking this ride with you and we wish we had tips like this when we were in your position. Thank you for joining us on the journey to finding a great job. We have come a long way since we started with the job search roadmap. We wish you the best of luck in your career.

Appendix 1 (Interview Template)

A. Company Information
1. Company Name:
2. Description (Wikipedia):
3. Industry:
4. Divisions (if applicable):

5. Locations:
6. Size:
7. Google News articles on it:
8. Two major products (if applicable):

B. Job Information
1. Technical requirements:
2. Individual(Non-technical) qualities required:

C. Your Qualifications
1. Technical requirements that you possess from B.1:
2. Proof (Project example) that you possess B.1:
3. Non-technical requirements that you possess from B.2:

4. Proof (experience) that you possess B.2:
5. How you plan to make up for it:

D. Your Interest

1. What made you apply for position B.1?

2. Why did you apply for this company A.1?

3. What attracts you to industry A.3?

E. Your Questions

1. Determine weaknesses of Products A.8. Ask questions about how weaknesses are overcome.

2. How is Products A.8 better than previous products? Cost comparison.

3. Determine future plans for the company and industry. If unable to figure it out, ask what they are.

4. What's your long term vision for the department?

F. Generic Questions

Note down other questions that you want to ask (location, number of candidates, time for decision etc.)

1.

Appendix 2(Sample Interview Template-Filled)

A. Company Information

Name: Coca-Cola

Description (Wikipedia): Coca-Cola Company is a company that produces and sells sugary, carbonated drinks for the globe. It includes several varieties such as Fanta, Sprite, Coca-Cola etc. It also produces and sells several varieties of snacks and drinks.

Industry: Food Industry

Divisions (if applicable):

Locations: Atlanta, Georgia.

Size: $9 billion

Google News:

Two major products (if applicable): Coke, Monster, Schweppes, Diet Coke, Capri Sun

B. Job Information

Technical requirements:
Fluidics theory and practice
Quality planning tools
Design for manufacturability (PFMEA / test automation)
Cost/Benefit of tradeoff decisions
Reviewing designs for improvements
Prioritize risks with respect to theory

Individual (Non-technical) qualities required:
Drive Innovation
Communication with stakeholders
Ownership of projects

C. Your Qualifications

Technical requirements that you possess from B.3: working with completing designs in CAD to meet customer requirements

Use of DFMEA to optimize product quality/reliability
Advanced problem solving and data analysis skills to optimize quality of product

Proof (Project example) that you possess B.3:
Project at Gifford Engineering regarding Mapper system. Talk about leading project through design, manufacturing and final delivery
Talk about problem solving at current project

Non-technical requirements that you possess from B.4:
Drive Innovation
Communication with stakeholders
Ownership of projects

Proof (experience) that you possess B.4:
Innovation
　　1. Digital Meisterbock
　　2. 3D Printing
　　3. BSAT Visual Presentation

Requirements from B.3/B.4 that you lack:
fluidics practical experience.

How you plan to make up for it: from previous experience, I am a very dynamic learner and can apply my skills to a new job.

D. Your Interest

4. **What made you apply for position B.1?** I am very interested in the position. I am passionate about innovation, design optimization and product improvement. My background, prior to this position, is one of product optimization. Experience at Continental/ Engineous Software and Masters' indicate this. My current position has given me good experience in understanding the limitations of the manufacturing process
    b. Enjoy product design and optimization
    c. Enjoy an environment of innovation
    d. Problem solving experience

5. **Why did you apply for this company A.1?** Coca-Cola is a large global corporation with a revenue of $9 billion with a lot of room for career growth. It is a more global company than Chrysler with more opportunities.

6. **What attracts you to industry A.3?** very global industry; with a lot of room for growth

E. Generic Questions

Note down other questions that you want to ask (location, number of candidates, time for decision etc.)
2. Q1: How long will it take to decide?
3. Q2: How do you decide which metrology equipment to use? Do you use roundness testers, etc.?
4. Q3: What are the common statistical process control methods that are used? Pareto charts, scatter plots, Latin Hypercube samples
5. Q4: What is the most common Regression method that you use? ANOVA Regression?

www.ingramcontent.com/pod-product-compliance
Lightning Source LLC
Chambersburg PA
CBHW071925290426
44110CB00013B/1475